W9-ALW-780

People of the Bible

The Bible through stories and pictures

The Prodigal Son

Copyright © in this format Belitha Press Ltd., 1983

Text copyright © Catherine Storr 1983

Illustrations copyright © Gavin Rowe 1983

Art Director: Treld Bicknell

First published in the United States of America 1983
by Raintree Publishers Inc.
310 West Wisconsin Avenue, Milwaukee, Wisconsin 53203
in association with Belitha Press Ltd., London.

Conceived, designed and produced by Belitha Press Ltd.,
2 Beresford Terrace, London N5 2DH

ISBN 0-8172-1982-X (U.S.A.)

Library of Congress Cataloging in Publication Data

Storr, Catherine.
      The prodigal son.

      (People of the Bible)
      Summary: A simple retelling of the New Testament
parable of the prodigal son.
      I. Prodigal son (Parable)—Juvenile literature. 2. Bible
stories, English—N.T. Luke. I. Rowe, Gavin. II. Title.
III. Series.
BT378.P8S76   1983   226′.409505   82-23011

ISBN 0-8172-1982-X

All rights reserved. No part of this book may be reproduced
or utilized in any form or by any means, electronic or
mechanical, including photocopying, recording, or by any
information storage and
retrieval system, without permission in writing
from the Publisher.

Printed in The United States of America.

4567891011121314   97 96 95 94 93 92 91 90 89 88 87

The Prodigal Son

Retold by Catherine Storr
Pictures by Gavin Rowe

Raintree Childrens Books
Milwaukee
Belitha Press Limited • London

Jesus called all the people to listen to him. Some of them muttered, "Look at this man! He is supposed to be so good, but he goes about with bad people who do wicked things. He even eats with them."

"Good people don't need me to help them," Jesus said. "Bad people do."

Then he told a story. "If a shepherd has a hundred sheep and one is missing, he leaves the ninety-nine who are safe, and he goes off to look for the one that is lost. When he's found it, he calls his friends and says, 'Isn't it wonderful? I've found the lost sheep!'"

"If a woman has ten pieces of money and loses one, she won't think about the other nine. She spends her time looking for the lost coin."

"It's like that with our father, God. When one bad man is sorry for the wicked things he's done, all the angels in heaven rejoice. It's more important to them than counting the people who have been good all their lives."

Then Jesus told another story about a man who had two sons. He loved them both, and he gave each of them half of everything he had.

The elder son stayed at home and helped his father.

The younger son took everything his father had given him, and he went off into a distant country. He spent all his money there, having a good time.

Before long he had no money left. He had
to get a job looking after pigs, and he had
nothing to eat except what the pigs left.

Then he thought, "Even the servants in
my father's house live better than this. I'll go
back home. I won't ask him to look after me
like a son, I don't deserve that. I'll be happy
being one of his servants."

So he went home. His father saw him coming from a long way off. He was so pleased to see him that he ran to hug him.

The son said, "Father, I'm sorry. Let me be one of your servants. I don't deserve to be your son any more."

But the father said to his servants, "Bring out a splendid robe for my son, a ring for his finger, and shoes for his feet."

The father went on, "Get a fat calf ready to make a feast. I thought my son was dead and that I'd never see him again. But look! He's alive, and he's here. Let's celebrate and be happy."

When the elder son saw all these preparations going on, he was angry.

"It isn't fair!" he said to his father. "I've been here with you all the time, and I've done everything you asked. But you never made such a fuss about me."

"It's true," his father said, "you have stayed here with me. I love you very much, and you can have anything you want that I can give you. But because your brother was lost, and now I've found him again, I have to be especially glad. Please be glad with me."

Many friends and relations came to the feast. There were dancers and musicians, and everyone rejoiced in the lost son's return.

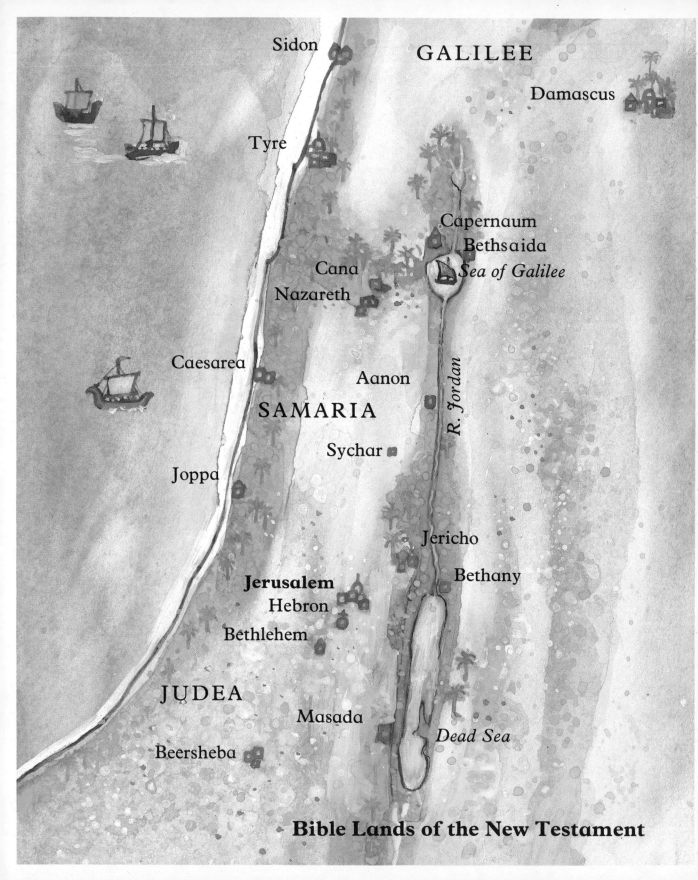

Bible Lands of the New Testament